Grandma's Hummingbird

by Christian Downey

illustrated by Durga Bernhard

Scott Foresman
is an imprint of

Glenview, Illinois • Boston, Massachusetts • Mesa, Arizona
Shoreview, Minnesota • Upper Saddle River, New Jersey

Every effort has been made to secure permission and provide appropriate credit for photographic material. The publisher deeply regrets any omission and pledges to correct errors called to its attention in subsequent editions.

Unless otherwise acknowledged, all photographs are the property of Pearson.

Photo locations denoted as follows: Top (T), Center (C), Bottom (B), Left (L), Right (R), Background (Bkgd)

Illustrations by Durga Bernhard

Photograph 16 Robert Harding World Imagery

ISBN 13: 978-0-328-39364-0
ISBN 10: 0-328-39364-9

1 2 3 4 5 6 7 8 9 10 V010 17 16 15 14 13 12 11 10 09 08

Sue lives with her family in New Mexico. They are members of the Zuni Indian tribe. They live in a pueblo, which is a village with houses made of sturdy bricks. These bricks are made in a special way and dried in the sun. Sue's house has a flat roof and is next to the Zuni River.

Sue's family lives off the land. Dad grows corn and other crops. He plants the corn in the spring and keeps the seeds watered. This is not easy because the land is very dry, so Dad waters the fields every day. In summer and fall, the corn grows very tall. Sue likes to hide in the cornfields, but Dad always finds her before dark.

Sue loves when it rains. She likes to sit inside and listen to the raindrops. Dad is also glad for the rain because it helps the crops grow.

"Will the corn grow tall and strong this year, Dad?" asks Sue.

"If it keeps raining, it will!"

"Has corn always grown here?" asks Sue.

"Yes, we have always grown crops here. Zunis are good farmers," says Dad.

Sometimes Sue gets to help Mom and Grandma make jewelry to sell to visitors. People come from all over to the pueblo where they live to buy their goods. Grandma also carves little animals out of stones and shells. She adds feathers and beads to them. Zunis believe that these animals will bring good luck. Grandma carves snakes, wolves, birds, and lions.

Today Grandma is carving a new animal. Sue peeks over Grandma's shoulder as she works, her hands making delicate strokes.

"What are you making?" Sue asks.

"A hummingbird," says Grandma. "Do you know the story of the magic hummingbird?"

"No," says Sue. "Tell me, please!"

"Once there was a hummingbird with a rainbow coat," says Grandma.

"He took off his coat to go into the village. There, he fell in love with the chief's daughter, and she fell in love with him too. The hummingbird hoped to marry her."

"The others in the tribe were mad," Grandma continues. "Without his rainbow coat, the hummingbird was plain. The people of the village did not like this and were very mean to him. One day, he put his rainbow coat back on. He flew away from the village to where the parrots lived. He came back with a golden cage. Inside the cage were bright birds. The hummingbird planted seeds all around the cage. When the tribe found the birdcage the next day, there were plants and vegetables growing up around it. There were also extra seeds for planting."

"Seeds for crops!" says Sue.

"Yes!" says Grandma. "The hummingbird had given them enough food for a year. Everyone was sorry for being mean to the hummingbird who had helped them. Now, I'm carving this beautiful hummingbird for a special person."

"For me?" asks Sue excitedly.

"I'm not telling!" laughs Grandma.

Sue likes to listen to Grandma's tales, and she likes to inquire about the Zuni past too. Grandma knows a lot about Zuni history.

Sue also helps her mother and father. Her father is building a river dam that will hold water. Their land gets very little rain, but the crops still need a lot of water. Sue hopes the dam will help her father grow more corn.

Sue's mother makes pottery. She fires the pots outside, next to the pueblo. She puts the clay pots under special branches that will not catch on fire. This way, the pots get hot enough to become hard ceramic, but the fire is very small. For hundreds of years, this is the way the Zuni tribes have made pottery.

Everyone in Sue's pueblo works together. Community is a big part of Zuni life. Sue's family likes to help others. They give food and gifts to others, and they help the tribe build and grow.

"If we are good to the land, it will be good to us," Sue's grandmother teaches her.

"If we all work together, more gets done!" says Sue proudly.

After the crops have grown, Sue helps Grandma mix the corn and flour they will use to bake corn bread. As they work, Grandma tells Sue stories. When they run out of corn, Sue goes to get more. When she comes back, her grandmother has a surprise.

"Sue, will you get me the big spoon?" Grandma asks.

"Sure!" replies Sue.

Sue goes to the table, and next to the spoon is a gift. It is the hummingbird Grandma carved!

“Thank you! Thank you!” says Sue.

“You are a very special girl,” says Grandma, receiving a big hug from Sue.

“Will it bring me good luck?” asks Sue.

“Of course. I made it for you!” says Grandma.

Grandma tells Sue that the Zuni believe the carved stone animals keep the tribe safe. Sue feels special because of her new gift.

That night, Sue goes to bed early. She puts the hummingbird under her pillow so it will bring her good luck. Grandma comes to tuck her in and to tell her a story.

"Grandma, will I have stories to tell like you someday?" Sue wonders.

"You will have even more! It's your job to pass them on," says Grandma.

"When I grow up, I want to be just like you," says Sue.

"Good night, sweet Sue," says Grandma.

Zuni Traditions

The Zuni tribe has held on to its traditions for years. The Zuni were one of many groups that first lived on the land that now forms Arizona and New Mexico. They still live on the same land today. They have grown corn for over two thousand years.

Zunis speak English, but they also speak their own language. Today, the Zuni people are trying to make sure their language and traditions are kept alive.

A Zuni craftsman making turquoise jewelry